Father Means Love

FATHER MEANS LOVE *Warmhearted Writings About a Very Special Person*

Selected by Barbara Kunz Loots
Illustrated by Dennis Lawrence Bellile

Hallmark Editions

Acknowledgments: "My Little Child" from Collected Poems and Plays by Rabindranath Tagore.
Copyright 1913 by Macmillan Publishing Co., Inc., renewed 1941 by Rabindranath Tagore.
Reprinted with permission of Macmillan Publishing Co., Inc. and the Trustees of the Tagore
Estate and Macmillan, London and Basingstoke. "The Most Gigantic of Joys" from A Halo for
Father by Joseph A. Breig. Copyright 1953 by The Bruce Publishing Company. Reprinted with
permission of Glencoe Publishing Co., Inc. "My Dad and I" from Runny Days, Sunny Days by
Aileen Fisher. Copyright 1958 by Aileen Fisher. Published by Abelard-Schuman Limited. By
permission of the author. "Innocent Bystander" from Nights With Armour by Richard Armour.
Copyright © 1958 by Richard Armour. Used with permission of the publisher, McGraw-Hill
Book Company. "My Beau Ideal" from Tallulah-My Autobiography by Tallulah Bankhead.
Copyright © 1952 by Tallulah Bankhead. Reprinted by permission of William Morris Agency,
Inc. "A Father's Advice" from The Crack-Up by F. Scott Fitzgerald. Copyright 1945 by New
Directions Publishing Corporation. Reprinted by permission of New Directions Publishing
Corporation and The Bodley Head. "Kids' Questions" from "Daddy, Can You Gargle With Your
Mouth Closed?" by Thomas Bolton. Reprinted by permission from the February 1975 issue of
Reader's Digest.

No need to teach a bird to fly
or teach a tree to touch the sky
or teach the sun to shine above
or teach a father
how to love.

Robin St. John

In the eyes of his children a father is everything wonderful — he is security and understanding and loyalty and love, and no moment of the day is happier than when someone shouts — "Dad's home!"

Katherine Nelson Davis

THE MOST GIGANTIC OF JOYS

Much is written in poetic praise of motherhood. Little is written in that vein of fatherhood. The father is generally regarded as a kind of noble but weary beast of burden, silently enduring the tedium of providing for his family. Of the rewards of fatherhood almost nothing is said. Yet I suspect that the most gigantic of all human joys are experienced by fathers.

Joseph A. Breig

WHAT KIND OF FATHER
WOULD I LIKE TO BE?

When I was a boy I used to ask myself, "What do I want to be when I grow up?" My answer was always based on what seemed the most exciting: an astronaut, a cowboy, a fireman. As I grew older my answers were decided by more important values. I guess it's only natural for a son to think about what kind of father he would like to be.

My thoughts are the same now as they were then. I hope I will be as willing to listen as I am to give advice. I hope I'll be strong yet never afraid to show gentleness. I hope I'll always see the humorous side of things, even though it sometimes means laughing at myself.

I hope I'll earn my family's respect, and respect each member of my family. I hope I'll have my family's love — and always deserve it. What I'm really saying is I hope I'll be a father like *my* father.

Steve Finken

FATHER'S CHAIR

Father loves his chair,
with its arms that make perfect horses
for busy cowgirls and cowboys,
and its tall, sturdy back
that provides a hideout for tired outlaws
and a fort for small soldiers.
Father loves his chair,
with its plaid covering
of mustard yellow and chocolate brown
that doesn't show late-night spills
or scuffing from dangling feet.
Father loves his chair,
with its plump cushions wide enough
for him and his children
and maybe a kitten to curl up in together.
Father loves his chair,
for it's a place where love surrounds him
when he's sitting there.

Tina Hacker

MY BEAU IDEAL

Daddy, graduate of two colleges, used to
say: "If you know your Bible, Shakespeare,
and can shoot craps, you have a liberal
education." To me he was a fusion
of Santa Claus, Galahad, D'Artagnan and
Demosthenes. He was the gallant, the
romantic, the poet, above all the actor.

Tallulah Bankhead

POEM

My father could not make a poem,
But setting his course by yonder pine,
Straight and true he plowed a line
Across the field. My father could not
Juggle words, but with the birth
Of golden wheat in summer sun,
He coaxed a poem out of the earth.

Mary Ferrell Dickinson

DEFINITION OF A DAD

If he's wealthy and prominent, and you stand in awe of him, call him "Father." If he sits in his shirt sleeves and suspenders at a ball game and picnic, call him "Pop." If he wheels the baby carriage and carries bundles meekly, call him "Papa" (with the accent on the first syllable). If he belongs to a literary circle and writes cultured papers, call him "Papa" (with the accent on the last syllable).

If, however, he makes a pal of you when you're good, and is too wise to let you pull the wool over his loving eyes when you're not; if, moreover, you're sure no other fellow you know has quite so fine a father, you may call him "Dad."

William B. Franklin

HELPING DAD

My boy likes to sleep late,
But he'd get up at dawn
To help me fix something
Or mow the lawn.

And many's the time
I've been tempted to say,
"Thanks, Son, but you'd only
Be in the way."

Then I stop and recall
That when I was a lad
The thing I loved most
Was helping my dad.

No matter the task,
He'd let me "help" do it,
And though small help or none,
Well, I never knew it.

So I let my son help me
And praise what he does,
Trying to be half the dad
My father was.   *M. R. Hurley*

OUR TEAM

A father is like a coach. He sees you through your spring training. He shows you the fundamentals. He knows the rules of the game — its penalties and rewards. Sometimes when you fumble or stumble or strike out, he may smile a bit. But he always teaches you how to recover and how to touch all the bases. When you score a touchdown, hit a home run or cross the finish line, he's the first to cheer. He makes you glad you're on his team. *Henry Skiba*

KIDS' QUESTIONS

Daddy, if the sun is burning, why isn't there any smoke? Why do we take the flag down at night, when we just have to put it up again in the morning? If hours are bigger than minutes, why aren't the little hands minutes and the big hands hours?

Most of us assume that when children ask such questions they are interested in the correct answers, and that it is our parental duty to provide same. How else, we ask ourselves, will the little tykes get into college? Until recently I thought so, too. But then, just this year, while wrestling with questions asked by my own three girls, I made a major conceptual breakthrough: Children don't give a hoot about receiving an accurate response to most of their questions. What they are *really* looking for is cheap entertainment.　　*Thomas Bolton*

INNOCENT BYSTANDER

My little daughter loves to stand
  Beside me when I shave,
And, conscious of my gallery,
  I'm careful to behave.

She loves to see the lather foam,
  To hear the razor scrape.
She loves the way I screw my face
  In each unlovely shape.

She's spellbound by the gear I spread
  Upon the bathroom shelf,
But most of all she waits around
  In hopes I'll cut myself.

       Richard Armour

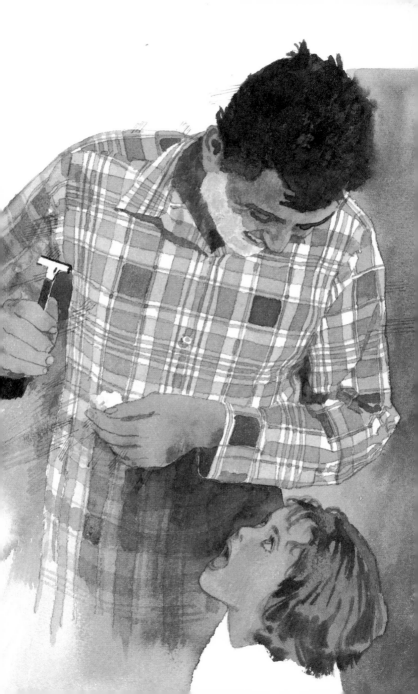

HEART-SONG FOR MY FATHER

All my life I wore your love,
Silk scarf about my throat.
A father to a daughter
Is a silver note,
A talisman against all tears,
Fortress against fright,
Shield against the deepest hurt,
Candle in the night.
Most of all, my dragons fell
At just the thought of you,
Steadfast the haven of your heart
To last my lifetime through.

Gladys McKee

No one really understands
    just how a father knows
Exactly what a boy will need
    to guide him as he grows.
No one really understands
    the way a father can
Exactly what it takes
    to turn a boy into a man.

George Webster Douglas

DAD AT THE BARBECUE

Mother is trying
To keep the rolls warm,
Dad's late with the steaks,
According to form!
The potatoes are burned
(And so is Dad's thumb),
We kids are so hungry
Our stomachs are numb.
Then, just as we're desperately
Sneaking a treat,
Dad hollers, "Hey!
You guys ready to eat?!"
The hood is lifted,
The smoke is unfurled,
Dad's at the barbecue,
All's right with the world!

Barbara Burrow

MY LITTLE CHILD

Say of him what you please, but I know my child's failings.

   I do not love him because he is good, but because he is my little child.

   How should you know how dear he can be when you try to weigh his merits against his faults?

   When I must punish him, he becomes all the more a part of my being.

   When I cause his tears to come, my heart weeps with him.

   I alone have a right to blame and punish, for he only may chastise who loves.

Rabindranath Tagore

To show a child what has once delighted you, to find the child's delight added to your own, so that there is now a double delight seen in the glow of trust and affection, this is happiness.

J. B. Priestly

THIS IS A FATHER

This is a father —
Strength and gentleness
And rough sweaters with
Comforting shoulders inside,
Tender eyes that
Crinkle in the corners,
Warm strong hands
That can build a birdhouse
Or make a kite
Or mend a doll buggy
Or lift a child
High — high — higher
Into a world of leaves and sunshine
Where one can see
A nest of robins.
A father is made up of
Quiet understanding,
Shared security,
Unquestioning love.

Doris Chalma Brock

WATCHING THE CIRCUS

What a thrill it was to see the clowns,
The huge, gray elephants, too,
The lion tamer with all those cats,
The crowds and the hullabaloo,
The high wire acts with the pretty girls,
The bicycling chimps riding round,
The midgets with their miniature cars,
The trick horses pawing the ground...

Oh, I was a thrilled, enchanted beholder
Watching the circus from Daddy's shoulder!

Katherine Nelson Davis

MY FATHER KNEW

My father knew what a woman should be, so he brought me up with spirit and style and, most of all, love.

I remember, in my young years, being treated with all the dignity proper to a lady and all the vigor proper to a pup. I was bounced, jounced, wrestled, rumpled. I was also praised in pretty dresses.

My father taught me how to hammer a nail, hook a worm, write a poem, hang a picture. He taught me "go-zintas" (otherwise known as long division) and how to be friends with boys.

I remember how I used to stand poised on the edge of some high bank or playground precipice, urged on by my father's hearty, "Jump! I'll catch you!" I always jumped. He always caught. And my life has been full of confident leaps of one kind or another ever since.

Barbara Kunz Loots

Sometimes only a father is truly aware
   Of his daughter's needs and wants and cares
And what she dreams and how she grows...
   Sometimes only a father knows.

Marjorie Frances Ames

My son is 7 years old. I am 54. It has taken me a great many years to reach that age. I am more respected in the community, I am stronger, I am more intelligent, and I think I am better than he is. I don't want to be a pal, I want to be a father. *Clifton Fadiman*

To be popular at home is a great achievement. The man who is loved by the house cat, by the dog, by the neighbor's children and by his own wife is a great man, even if he has never had his name in *Who's Who*.

Thomas Dreier

DADDY LOVES MOMMY

"Daddy loves Mommy."
"How do you know?"
"This morning I heard him telling her so.
She was out in the kitchen,
And Daddy came down
And swooped her up and swung her around.
That's when he said it — and Mommy smiled,
And Daddy held her a long, long while.
That's how I know for certain it's true
That Daddy loves Mommy."
"I'm glad."
"Me, too."

Barbara Burrow

For a person in rugged health who is not particularly dressed up and does not want to write a letter or read the newspaper, we can imagine few diversions more enjoyable than to have a child turned loose upon him.

Heywood Broun

A dad knows how to give his children good advice. But he also knows that his children need to think things out for themselves and form their own conclusions. There are times when they must do the talking, times when they can really use a friend who will just listen...and understand.

Edward Cunningham

A FATHER ANSWERS

Explaining things to my little boy gives me a real sense of fellowship with the millions of fathers down through the centuries who have struggled to find answers for their children. I'm sure we have a lot in common — that dad who lived in 500 B.C. and me. Except I'm a little luckier. My favorite answer to "Why?" is "Let's look it up."

John Gray

A FATHER'S ADVICE

Things to worry about: Worry about courage/ Worry about cleanliness/ Worry about efficiency/ Worry about horsemanship....

Things not to worry about: Don't worry about popular opinion/ Don't worry about dolls/ Don't worry about the past/ Don't worry about the future/ Don't worry about growing up/ Don't worry about anybody getting ahead of you/ Don't worry about triumph/ Don't worry about failure unless it comes through your own fault/ Don't worry about mosquitoes/ Don't worry about flies/ Don't worry about insects in general/ Don't worry about parents/ Don't worry about boys/ Don't worry about disappointments/ Don't worry about pleasures/ Don't worry about satisfactions.

F. Scott Fitzgerald

LIKE MY DAD

Lord, make me something like my dad;
       Give me a little of his will,
That good old stubbornness he had
       That helped him up the hardest hill,
Content to wait and work and fight,
Believing always he was right.

Douglas Malloch

MY DAD AND I

My dad and I
made shavings fly:
we built a shelf for books,
and planed a door
and patched the floor
and put up several hooks,
and plugged a leak
and oiled a squeak
and got the toaster wired.
I hoped we might
keep on all night...
but Dad got *awfully* tired.

Aileen Fisher

A SWING TO REMEMBER

It was the nicest swing to dream in,
To think and plan in, too,
And I didn't have to treat it
Like one all fine and new...
It was just a plain old car tire
Smoothed slick by miles of wear,
And it curved down in the middle
Like our old porch chair...
It wasn't that it went so high,
And it didn't look like much,
But it had an easy sway to it
That started with a touch...
But what made that swing the best swing
Anyone has ever had
Was that it had been made for me
With special love, by dad.

M. R. Hurley

THE DEMOCRATIC FAMILY
...SORT OF

When I was growing up, my father's favorite words were "Let's vote on it." Our family of three voted on just about everything, from what TV programs we watched to what time I should go to bed. My parents definitely had the upper hand in this system...that is, until the twins were born. When they were six and we voted to buy a horse, I thought the tables had turned at last. Undaunted, my father smiled and announced, "The voting age in this family has just been raised — to eighteen!"

Blanche Weiss

No matter how many waves
    come rushing to the shore,
there is still another
    and yet one more.
Such is the love in a father's heart.

Tina Hacker

Set in Weiss Roman, a typeface designed in 1926
by Emil Rudolf Weiss, eminent European artist
who contributed much to the world's book and graphic arts.
Weiss was a painter, illustrator, designer,
calligrapher, typographer, poet, writer and teacher.

Designed by Lilian Weytjens.